BIX BEIDERBECKE
Jazz Age Genius

Notable Americans

BIX BEIDERBECKE
Jazz Age Genius

David R. Collins

MORGAN
REYNOLDS
Incorporated

Greensboro

BIX BEIDERBECKE: *Jazz Age Genius*

Copyright © 1998 by David R. Collins

Library of Congress Cataloging-in-Publication Data
Collins, David R.
  Bix Beiderbecke : jazz age genius / David R. Collins —1st ed.
    p. cm. — (Notable Americans)
  Includes bibliographical references and index.
  Summary: A biography of the cornet player from Davenport, Iowa, who helped raise jazz
to a respected musical form and who was inducted into the International Jazz Hall of Fame
in 1997.
  ISBN 1-883846-36-6 (hc.)
    1. Beiderbecke, Bix, 1903-1931—Juvenile literature. 2. Cornet players—United
States—Biography—Juvenile literature. 3. Jazz musicians—United States—Biography—
Juvenile literature. [1. Beiderbecke, Bix, 1903-1931. 2. Cornet players. 3. Musicians.
4. Jazz.] I. Title II. Series.
ML3930. B42C6 1998
788.9' 6165' 092—dc21
[B]

                                                                98-19824
                                                                    CIP
                                                                 AC MN

Printed in the United States of America
First Edition

*This book is dedicated to
Rich Johnson who knows how to hit
just the right notes in a musical score
and in a friendship.*

Acknowledgments

*For photographs used in this book,
the author wishes to gratefully acknowledge
Kay Runge, Rochelle Murray,
and the
Special Collections Center of the Davenport Public Library,
and jazz enthusiast
Rich Johnson of the Bix Beiderbecke Memorial Society.*

Contents

Bix Beiderbecke

Chapter One

The Beat Begins

By the time he was seven years old, Leon Bix Beiderbecke was sure of three things.

First of all, he hated being called "Leon." It was a name selected for no particular reason. His birth certificate listed Leon Bix Beiderbecke, born March 10, 1903, in Davenport, Iowa. "Bix" was his father's nickname as well as his older brother's, but neither Bismark Herman Beiderbecke nor Charles Burnette Beiderbecke had the name "Bix" officially listed on their birth certificates like Leon Bix did. The boy discarded the name "Leon" at an early age, and "Bix" became the name he used throughout his life, although family and friends often called him "Bixie" and "Bickie."

Second, Bix liked the house he grew up in. The two-story wooden structure at 1934 Grand Avenue in Davenport contained more rooms and closets than the boy could count, offering perfect hide-and-seek spots for Bix, his older sister Mary Louise and older brother Burnie. Agatha Beiderbecke enforced the adage "Cleanliness is next to godliness," keeping both her home and children spotless. Not only was the house on Grand Avenue a child's castle, it boasted a magnificent wraparound porch, perfect for running races all seasons of the year. An adventurous Bix occasionally journeyed beyond the house and yard.

Neighborhood children were told to be on alert for the wayfaring tot, and his mother always had a nickel ready for anyone bringing him home. Sometimes the boy crossed the trolley tracks in front of the family home to the playground of John Tyler Elementary School across the street. At first he watched the other kids playing, but soon he was swinging a bat with force and fire and running the bases like a little steam engine.

The third thing Bix was sure of was that he loved music. No doubt, growing up with a mother whose hands flew across the piano keyboard with grace and precision contributed to that early love for sound. Debussy, Chopin, Beethoven—the boy heard the composers' names and saw them printed on sheet music. But it was not the names that were important. It was the notes the composers had created, the sounds that brought joy and happiness and sadness too. Before he could walk, Bix pushed his heels into the floor carpeting as his mother played, often ending up wedged under a chair or table. By the time he was two, he was plunking out the melody to "Oh, Mr. Dooley." It did not matter that he couldn't reach the keyboard. He stretched his hands above his head to play the song. When his

By age five, Bix often played the piano before his friends and family in this "Anchors Aweigh!" outfit.

kindergarten classmates gathered to celebrate Bix's fifth birthday, he entertained them with one-fingered versions of "Pop Goes the Weasel!" and "Yankee Doodle Came to Town."

As an executive with the East Davenport Coal and Lumber Company, Bismark Beiderbecke enjoyed a place of prominence within the city's social community. His family shared the spotlight, and the story of "Little Bixie" as a "musical wonder" made its way onto the pages of the local newspaper, the *Davenport DailyDemocrat:*

> "...He plays every selection that he learns as completely in the bass and treble clef as it is written. In fact, so acute is his ear for music that as his mother plays a piece in another key than that in which "Bickie" has always played it, the child will sit down and play the piece in exactly the same key with proper bass accompaniment."

It was not only the way Bix learned new music, it was the way he performed it. Most young pianists his age focused intently on the sheet music before them or the keyboard and their fingers. Not Bix. His gaze wandered about the room, occasionally stopping to stare at an object. But his concentration was totally absorbed by the music he was playing. His fingers often improvised, speeding up the tempo or slowing it, each time revealing a different interpretation or mood. He delighted neighbors and family friends with his playing, usually leaving their homes with a pocketful of nickels for his efforts.

Bismark and Agatha Beiderbecke spent many hours discussing the best ways of handling their young musical prodigy. One

Bix developed scarlet fever and missed the entire third grade. Here he poses with the tutor his family hired to help him keep up with his school work.

relative insisted that he needed lessons, that Bix's talent needed special guidance.

Before the Beiderbeckes got the chance to act on the advice, Bix came down with scarlet fever. He was dropped from the third grade roster at Tyler Elementary and ordered to stay inside the house. It was a major frustration for Bix, who enjoyed the neighborhood ball games and wrestling with his playmates. Agatha Beiderbecke tried to maintain a schedule of school lessons each day, occasionally enlisting the help of Bix's sixteen-year-old brother, Burnie, and thirteen-year-old sister, Mary Louise. But the two teen-agers had social lives of their own, and playing teacher to a younger brother was not among their favorite activities.

Agatha Beiderbecke reached out further in an effort to nurture her son's recognized musical talents. Professor Charles Grade was hired to give Bix professional piano lessons. Once a week, the accomplished instructor made the forty-mile drive from his home in Muscatine to the Beiderbecke home in Davenport.

The lessons started out with great expectations. Professor Grade arrived with sheet music in hand, delighted to perform the selections to the pleasure of his student and family members nearby. "Now practice," the teacher admonished young Bix. "We'll hear how it sounds next week."

The following week, Bix performed the assigned music exactly the way Professor Grade had played it. The boy hardly looked at the sheet music at all. The boy could hear a selection

The Beiderbecke house was at 1934 Grand Avenue in Davenport, Iowa.

once, and replay it note for note. But could he actually read the notes? No, the boy could simply memorize the sounds and play them back. This might have gone undetected, but sometimes Professor Grade made mistakes in his initial performance before the family. When Bix played the selection the following week, he played the same mistakes. Other times, he improved the selection, adding his own arrangement. The piano teacher shook his head woefully. He reported to Bix's parents that he did not believe he could teach their son anything further about the piano. He pronounced that Bix was obviously a gifted musician, but complained that he did not appreciate the importance of learning to read music and performing a piece as it was written. Later, this urge to alter the written music would become an important part of jazz music.

The bout with scarlet fever held Bix back a year in school. When he returned to third grade at Tyler Elementary in the fall of 1912, he found new faces. But he was even further behind than before. The only subject he excelled in was music, when he could share his talents at the piano. In the other subjects, he was hopelessly behind. Interest in school dipped.

As the years slipped by, Bix's world expanded beyond Grand Avenue and Tyler Elementary School. Davenport sat peacefully along the banks of the Mississippi River, a mighty snake of water in America's heartland that brought giant riverboats each summer.

On summer evenings the strains of the riverboat bands

Nine-year-old Bix and a pony rented to ride around the block.

drifted through the air, serenading much of the city. To young Bix Beiderbecke, the music was magic, exciting melodies and tunes that made feet tap and the body jump to a special beat. To others, the music brought a disturbing and dangerous quality to the clean climate of the people. Ministers warned their adult congregations to keep a careful eye on their children lest they be "whisked away in a wind of moral degradation."

Bismark and Agatha Beiderbecke listened closely to such warnings. They had been raised with strict European and Christian ethics. They were determined to shelter their three growing children from any corrupting influences.

But Bix was pulled by the riverboats to the Davenport levee, drawn there with friends eager for adventure. The giant crafts brought people from New Orleans and other places far away, and an aroma of life beyond the strict conservative lifestyle of the typical Davenporter.

There was no tone, rhythm, or sound quite like that of the steam calliope. Its notes poured and pounded into the air, accompanied by a band aboard each steamboat. It was fun music, a kind of sound that danced into the heart and soul of people, especially young people. Like a magnet, the lively bouncing tunes drew Bix and his buddies to the waterfront. Despite warnings from his mother and father, Bix secretly stole away to join the happy moments beside the Mississippi.

One July night Bix was late for supper. It had happened before, more than once or twice, especially when The Quincy,

The proud and serious Beiderbecke family in 1905. Right to left: Mary Louise (sister), Agatha (mother), Bix, Bismark Herman (father) and Charles Burnette "Burnie" (brother).

The St. Louis, or another of the massive riverboats was docked along the Davenport levee. But as minutes slipped into hours, the Beiderbecke family became more and more concerned. Then the telephone rang. It was a captain of a riverboat. Bix had stowed away on a riverboat. The boat was in Muscatine and apparently the boy was aboard when the craft had left Davenport that afternoon.

The Beiderbeckes were relieved that their son was not harmed. Then they were angry with him for causing them so much stress. But they could not help but smile when Bismark reported that the captain had also said that the young runaway played the calliope better than anyone he had ever heard. He would have liked to give Bix a job, but he was too young.

Chapter Two

New Notes

"Play that horn, Louie!"

It was a constant shout when young Louie Armstrong performed aboard one of the riverboats moored at the Davenport levee. The young black man from New Orleans mesmerized his audiences. The pure notes poured from his golden cornet like sounds from another world. Each time he raised his horn, his listeners clapped their hands and tapped their feet.

It was not Bix's nature to shout, clap, and tap. He was quiet, more reserved. But no one soaked up the sounds more than the kid from Grand Avenue. Whenever he managed to sneak aboard one of the riverboats, he planted himself as close to the band as he could, not missing a note. He studied Louie Armstrong's moves, his fingers pushing the cornet keys, his lips pressed against the mouthpiece, tilting his instrument this way and that, holding a note firm and tight, loving it or kicking it, caressing it or blaring it. Yes, this Louis Armstrong could play that horn—and he was only three years older than Bix! No one understood and appreciated each note more than the short kid with tousled hair with his deep brown eyes focused on the band before him. His friends joked that Bix's ears stuck out so he could hear the music better.

Bix didn't mind the kidding. He took the jeers and jibes of his classmates in school too. Bookwork failed to interest him. Algebra proved a special pain. Both Burnie and Mary Louise brought home good grades, receiving the praise of their pleased parents. But Bismark and Agatha Beiderbecke shook their heads at Bix's scores. The boy wanted to do better, to make his mother and father proud. Each term he promised to work harder. But a piano bench felt a lot better than the seat of a classroom desk.

Bix gained a bit more freedom when he reached his teens. There were still warnings about spending too much time down at the levee, but Bismark and Agatha Beiderbecke concluded that forbidding Bix to go was purposeless. No doubt, they would have liked their son to pursue a musical path filled with more classical compositions. Yet that was not to be. Bix heard a different beat and liked a "swingier" style.

When a friend announced he planned to sell his cornet, Bix showed quick interest. He didn't have the thirty-five dollars needed, so he negotiated. He agreed to pay fifteen dollars down and seven or eight dollars a month. The deal was accepted. Now, sounds of two musical instruments, the piano and the cornet, poured out of the Beiderbecke house. There were no complaints. The ear of young Bix Beiderbecke became better tuned every day, and his playing echoed the sounds that streamed into his

The graduation photo of eighth grade class at Tyler Elementary School in 1917. Bix is in the second row, far right.

head. It was good listening, especially on warm summer nights.

It was about this same time that sounds of a different kind were being heard far away. German leaders were building a mighty military machine. Factories ran twenty-four hours a day, turning out war implements. At first, President Woodrow Wilson managed to keep the United States out of the fighting overseas. But by 1917, that effort collapsed. America went to war.

Across the nation, young men enlisted. A sophomore at Iowa State College in Ames, Burnie Beiderbecke signed up. It was a tragic irony, for his grandfather had immigrated to America from Germany and adopted his new country as his own. Although there were still Beiderbeckes in Germany, the newcomers to America were loyal to the United States. Bismark Beiderbecke supported his son's decision.

Fourteen-year-old Bix was proud of his brother. He wrote to Burnie to tell him so. The boy also learned to play all the patriotic songs being released on sheet music and records.

After completing his basic military training, Burnie became an army instructor stationed in Kentucky. Just when it appeared he might be sent into battle, a peace agreement was signed. Burnie headed back home to Davenport in early December of 1918. With a part of his savings, he bought the family a windup Gramophone and several records. It was a special Christmas present—especially for Bix. Among the selections Burnie brought home were several records of a new kind of music called jazz. It did not take long before Bix was accompanying every one

The steamboat Washington was one of several owned by the Streckfus brothers that docked at the Davenport levee. The Streckfus Line employed many musicians, including the young Louis Armstrong. Bix managed to sneak aboard to hear the music.

of the jazz tunes on his cornet, blasting away with his horn one moment and softly crooning with it the next.

By the time he entered Davenport High, Bix had a wide circle of friends. Despite his weakness with academics, he displayed a quick wit and fun sense of humor. His 150 pounds stretched firmly over a 5'9" frame, a friendly smile appeared often, and his auburn hair framed a handsome face. He found himself a girlfriend, Vera Cox, whom he took ice-skating and to play tennis. Bix was a speed demon on the ice and a superb shot placer on the court. But it was at dances and parties that he grabbed his most appreciative audience.

He spent much of his time near the band that was playing and never turned down an invitation to play when a free cornet was available. Sometimes he got so caught up in playing he forgot Vera entirely. She simply found a ride home with someone else. It wasn't that Bix was rude. It was just that if he had to choose between a girl and his horn, the horn always came first.

The other kids liked Bix's music too. It had its own style, a rhythm and motion that forced the mind and body to keep time, to respond. It wasn't that every note he played was perfect—it wasn't. Yet he played with such energy and enthusiasm. "You couldn't keep your body still if you wanted to," one classmate observed. "Bix just reached inside you with his horn and shook you up."

Bix was never satisfied with his own playing. He replayed every bar in his mind, wanting to make it better. Sometimes he

At Davenport High School Bix (lower right corner) preferred extracurricular activities such as croquet to academics.

performed in school assembly programs, expanding his audience even further. His teachers complimented his playing, no doubt wishing he could handle his homework and exams with the same skill he displayed on his cornet.

News of the young horn player from Davenport High spread throughout the city. Amateur musicians in small bands invited Bix to sit in with them. It was a good way to pick up spending money, and Bix welcomed the chance to do that. He hated asking his parents, especially when he brought home such poor grades.

When Bix wasn't playing with a band, he and his buddies headed down to the river where they could play as loud as they wished. On hot summer days they headed out of town, always finding a cluster of trees where they could cut loose in the shade. Bix's seat was often empty at the family table at mealtimes, and his school desk was too, while he slept in from late night "jam" sessions in someone's basement or a nearby roadhouse.

Bix patiently listened to his parents' lectures about the importance of a good education, of choosing friends carefully, and of budgeting time well. Everything they said made perfect sense. He promised to change, to work harder, and to settle down. Yet, as soon as he got his cornet in his hands, music was all that mattered. Words were forgotten.

Not being able to read music proved a major problem at times for Bix. When a band buddy, Esten Spurrier, came to him with an offer for a band job—one that paid big bucks—Bix was excited. Unfortunately, the job required the musicians to have a union card. A date was set for auditioning. When the other musicians arrived, Bix was nervous. Everyone could read music but him! When the group started out playing together, they sounded good. But when each musician was asked to play individually with the pianist, the trouble began. Not knowing how to read the musical score on his bandstand, Bix also played the piano part he could hear. When told to play the cornet part, the high school boy fumbled. He was told to go home, study, and practice, and come back when he'd learned to read music.

Bix was crestfallen. It wasn't only for himself that he felt badly. His inability to read music had caused the band to lose the job. Bix hated letting anyone down.

Bix felt worst about his parents, however. How much he wanted to please them. He just never seemed able to do it, even after Agatha devoted time every night to make sure he passed botany. Bismark brought him to the East Davenport Fuel and Lumber Company to tour the business. Perhaps, just perhaps, the boy might see something about it he would like. It might move him to work harder in school so he could someday enjoy a worthwhile job.

Music was the major force that attracted Bix, and everyone knew what the life of a professional musician was like. It was one thing to enjoy playing an instrument as a pastime. But music was not a suitable career choice for young men from conservative Davenport, Iowa. Why, most professional musicians were of seedy character with an instrument in one hand and a bottle of booze in the other.

And the worst kind of music, the music that led even the best of individuals into a fast life of decay and corruption was this new jazz, precisely the kind of sound that Bix loved the most. The Davenport cornet player wasn't the only one who loved the sound. Jazz bands were popping up across the country, with the unique sound filling record after record pouring from New York City recording studios. It was like a fast-spreading disease.

There was an unusual kind of hypocrisy in towns along the Mississippi River. Like other riverboat stopping places, the people of Davenport flocked to hear jazz being played by King Oliver and all the other groups coming north out of New Orleans. But these same jazz fans were convinced the musicians who played the music were caught in tangled webs of personal destruction.

It was that kind of thinking that made Bismark and Agatha Beiderbecke take drastic action. Convinced that Bix could never achieve any kind of academic success at Davenport High, and equally certain his intense focus on jazz music would end in tragic consequences, his parents made a fateful decision. They decided to enroll Bix in Lake Forest Academy near Chicago, Illinois. Known for its high academic standards and enforced disciplinary rules, the male boarding school seemed like the best place for Bix. It was close enough for them to visit regularly, and Mary Louise was teaching only thirty-five miles away. She could help keep an eye on her younger brother.

It seemed like a perfect plan.

Chapter Three

"Go East Young Man, Go East!"

When seventeen-year-old Bix Beiderbecke arrived on the campus of Lake Forest Academy in September of 1920, he was determined to change his ways. Study—study—study—that would be his motto. The cornet would remain in its case except for special occasions.

Most of the other boys at Lake Forest hailed from Illinois, so Bix took the usual ribbing about being "a hayseed" from Iowa. "How did you get here?" one classmate asked. "Ride a cow?"

"Yup!" Bix replied, his eyes sparkling. "It was udderly delightful," he answered, drawing immediate respect with his quick wit. He made friends fast at Lake Forest, although he retained his reserved manner. Bix was never one to barge into a conversation or crash a party. Yet, once he felt at ease, he could tell a good story or cast sarcastic barbs at anyone tossing caustic quips in his direction.

Thanks to his parents, Bix was equally prepared with stylish clothing of the time. His closets and dresser drawers bulged with cardigan sweaters, starched white collared shirts, tweed jackets, and narrow short cuffed trousers. He parted his plastered-down hair just to the right of center, a popular style for young men of the time.

Certainly the red brick buildings of Lake Forest dotting the rich green grasses of the neatly groomed campus contrasted with the dark grim singular structure that had been his school home at Davenport High. "Learning thrives through cooperative effort" boasted one institution pamphlet, and one dozen Lake Forest instructors worked actively to bring that logo to life for the 129 students attending the school. "We will build your mind and your character," the school officials promised in writing. Bismark and Agatha Beiderbecke crossed their fingers and prayed that the pledge would come true.

Bix's junior year at Davenport High School had been a total disaster. He had flunked so many courses there was no chance he could enter Lake Forest as a senior. In fact, upon close examination of his records, he did not even qualify as a junior. Therefore, he was placed in the "lower middle" section, or the sophomore class. The entry level did not seem to bother Bix. He had learned to endure the stigma of academic underachievement.

Bix jumped into a whirlwind of activity at Lake Forest, signing up for intramural football, baseball, and, of course, the school orchestra. Among his classmates, Bix found a variety of music lovers, many of them skilled musicians. But few of them had fingers that whizzed over piano keys like Bix's and lips that fit that cornet mouthpiece like they were made together as one unit.

Making new friends at the boarding house called East House came easily to the amiable young fellow from Iowa. He became a regular fixture at the piano in the parlor, his audience growing every time he played. But when Edmund Rendtorff, the live-in faculty advisor at East House, visited one impromptu gathering and declared that studies came before socializing, the group dispersed. "Young Master Beiderbecke," the instructor offered, "Let us be sure your classroom notes are as complete and resounding as those you play on the piano." Bix nodded, backing away and hurrying to his room. But one night not long afterward, one of Bix's buddies had an idea. Why not take a night train into Chicago and hit a speakeasy or two?

For three years the country had existed under prohibition laws, governmental rules set in place to outlaw the manufacture and sale of alcoholic beverages. In many places and by many people, the laws were ignored. The speakeasy nightspot offered a place for folks to get together, have a few illegal drinks, and listen to a band. Some speakeasies were elegant, catering to Chicago's elite. But other speakeasies were located in smoke-filled basements, the rooms jumping and jiving with clinking mugs and glasses, with shouted conversations over the noise of a lively group of instrumentalists in the background.

Bix thought it sounded like fun. It was fun—so much fun that Bix got into a regular habit of heading south into the Windy City, spending hour after hour listening to any and every band he could. With friends or by himself, Bix enjoyed the Chicago nightlife. He became comfortable sipping a drink or two, the liquid flowing smoothly and leaving the teen-ager from Lake Forest with a warm feeling deep inside. Once you got inside the speakeasy, and if you had the cash, no one cared who you were or how old either. The concern about flunking math, of completing a science report, of presenting a speech—all these troubles and problems flew out the window.

Bix soaked up the speakeasy atmosphere. At seventeen, he was usually the youngest in the room. Many boys his age might have been a bit nervous. Every speakeasy boasted its share of undesirables, with the criminal element in Chicago running the illegal booze syndicate. But it didn't seem to bother Bix that he was a couple hundred miles from home in Davenport, far away from his family and friends. All he needed was music. It surrounded him with security, a sense of feeling safe from any danger. In each speakeasy, Bix's gaze fixed on the musicians, their nimble hands and fingers picking out the notes, their puffing chests, their sweaty faces aglow, their feet tapping the rhythm. Bix's fingers softly drummed on the table near the band, his head bouncing slightly, keeping perfect time, only closing his eyes when a horn player cut loose with a few special bars of music, or a drummer pounded his sticks like he would never play again. Oh, yeah, this was living at its best. Minutes slipped into hours quickly, and then he caught a train back to Lake Forest, his head still filled with the magic of the music pounding away.

Back at school Bix s situation grew worse. Why did algebra have to be so complicated? Who would ever use the stuff anyway? And who cared about some old guy named Silas Marner and his gold coins? The Gettysburg Address was a great speech, of course, but what was the purpose in memorizing it. Bix struggled at Lake Forest Academy just like he had struggled at Davenport High. Instructors tried private tutoring sessions, and they tried to ignore the signs of regular hangovers that Bix could not hide. "The kid has music in his veins," one instructor observed. "He's in his own world."

It was no secret on campus that Bix loved music and that he was an excellent musician. While the other boys dined on the institutional meals at the boarding school, Bix was often invited to homes of staff members and other private citizens in the area. He repaid their generosity with an hour or two of piano selections after dinner. He knew most of his hosts and hostesses' requests by heart, but if he didn't, they only had to hum or whistle a few bars. Bix picked the rest up by ear.

Although the boy from Davenport raced up and down the keyboard with ease, he considered himself a horn man first. Some musicians, such as Louie Armstrong, had replaced the cornet with the trumpet. To Bix, the horn would always be a cornet. With classmates Cy Welge on drums and Sid Stewart on a C-melody saxophone, Bix set up a band to play for dances.

One of the Cy-Bix band's first bookings was the Halloween dance at Lake Forest. The group set up on a small balcony in the school gym that had been decorated with corn stalks, pumpkins and autumn leaf branches. Girls from Ferry Hall, a nearby elite boarding school for girls, were imported under the watchful eye of their headmistress, Miss Jane Tremain. She joined Lake Forest's headmaster, John Wayne Richards, to chaperon. All went well until intermission. Bix then decided to speed up the tempo, his cornet tones rolling into a wild and rollicking number that had the student dancers spinning and gyrating. They loved the sound, but it was too much for the flustered Richards, who quickly headed to the band location and demanded a return to more sedate offerings.

The music returned to its more restrained rhythm for the rest of the evening. But Bix was satisfied. He'd given his peers a taste of fresh jazz sounds, and they'd loved it. Bix's letters home to Davenport emphasized his efforts to keep good grades. "I'm really trying in Eng. Hist.," he wrote to his parents, "but it sure is hard for me—so damn much to remember and I sure have a lank of a memory."

He had no trouble remembering the way to the speakeasies in Chicago. He took a special interest in the Rhythm Kings playing in Friars' Inn. They had a smooth style, with trumpeter Paul Mares lending his own personal style and class to each number. The visitor from Lake Forest was too wrapped up in the music to notice others enjoying the fun of the Friars' layout. Mobsters Al Capone, Dion O'Banion, and Johnny Torrio were regulars at the place too, but they were more interested in how fast the cheap liquor was flowing than what the band was playing.

Louis Armstrong was one of the early jazz greats Bix heard in the speakeasys of Chicago while he attended Lake Forest Academy.

As for Bix, he started making friends among the groups he visited. Sometimes they asked him to mix it up a bit with them. He carried his cornet mouthpiece with him. The boy was always willing to slide onto a piano bench or grab a horn and show off his stuff. Band members dubbed him "Magic Fingers, Jr." and wondered how his hands moved so fast on the keyboard. Still others nicknamed him "Sweet Lips" for the way his mouth fit that cornet mouthpiece.

Now and then, Lake Forest brought a band onto the campus for a dance and concert. When Bix was spotted, the shout went up—"Hey, Bix!"—and an embarrassed but proud smile appeared on the boy's face.

Soon Bix began riding the night train farther south into the city. The black jazz bands played in speakeasies there, and Bix liked to compare and contrast the sounds of every group he heard.

When he returned to campus, he pulled out his own horn and tried a bit of this and that. He wanted his own style. The Rhythm Kings were certainly worthy of imitation. They swung with a smooth beat, neatly mixing sounds of old Southern spirituals with a slip and sliding movement. Yes, Bix was bringing jazz to the Lake Forest campus—whether they wanted it there or not.

Some definitely did not. Bix was playing with different bands, hitting area high school dances and mixers. An engagement at Ferry Hall turned into a disaster. The infamous Miss Jane Tremain, who had brought her girls to Lake Forest for the previous Halloween party, hired Bix's group for an engagement at her school. This time Bix cut loose with even greater gusto, turning the dancers into a wild collection of quick-stepping, hip-slapping grinders. She insisted the band provide a more sedate type of music. Shaking his head in disappointment, Bix returned to his band and reluctantly slowed the tempo and softened the sound.

Concerned letters from home further dampened Bix's spirits. Lake Forest officials kept close contact with the Beiderbeckes back in Davenport. Not only were Bix's grades low, reports of missing classes and staying out until early in the morning disturbed Bismark and Agatha. What was this hold that music had over their son? Why couldn't he stay focused on his schoolwork first, and put everything else second?

To Bix, the answer was easy. Music was a joy, a challenge, another world. There were 101 ways of sharing a mood, creating an emotion, touching a feeling. There was not one solution, but many avenues of pursuing the right refrain, the best chord, the perfect notes. If only others could understand.

The last straw came for Headmaster Richards in the spring of 1922. When he contacted Bix about hiring his band to play for the junior prom, Bix politely refused. His group already had a booking for the night—in Gary, Indiana, on the other side of Chicago. "You can't play for your own school because you're already playing for another?" Richard shook his head in disgust and disappointment.

Richards immediately imposed restrictions on Bix's band, limiting them to on-campus performances. The band members were angry. They were making some good money playing for high school dances and other engagements. Their name was being established and they dreamed of becoming a big-time band. The other instrumentalists at Lake Forest thought it was unfair too.

The disgruntled boys of Lake Forest decided to stage a protest. One morning a group of them gathered in a dorm room where they mixed a concoction of Ed Pinaud's Face Lotion (eighty-five percent alcohol!) with water. While lying flat on their backs, they gulped the mixture down. It tasted awful and smelled worse. In fact, the boys clothespinned their noses while they swallowed the liquid. Then they hurried off to chapel to play for the morning services attended by the faculty and student body. By the time the group reached the familiar solemn tones of "Rock of Ages" in the program, the alcoholic mixture had kicked in. Bix gave the signal and the instrumentalists burst into a Dixieland Jazz version of the traditional hymn. Headmaster Richards could not believe his ears. He stopped the music and ordered the building cleared—except for the musicians.

With the steely manner of a prosecuting attorney, Richards demanded the name of the ringleader of the protest. He already had a good idea who it was. No one responded, therefore he put the entire group on probation.

Bix felt miserable. He had not intended to get anyone in trouble. Why couldn't people understand that jazz music was not unhealthy or unholy or anything else sinful? It was a sound, a special sound, that made his mind and body beat with rhythm, his heart pound with power, his mind float into ecstasy.

The following Sunday morning the staff at Lake Forest met with Headmaster Richards in emergency session. Bix Beiderbecke was the topic, and those present shared their experiences and impressions.

Most knew that he was a fine musician and respected his talent. But there was the business of his incomplete assignments, poor test grades, missed classes, and a general disinterest in school. They had noticed his hangovers too. Might he lead other students along the same reckless road?

Edmund Rendtorff, the East Hall advisor, recounted the nights he had found Bix missing from bed check. Bix was always apologetic, sincerely sorry about causing any trouble. Yet within the week, he was back doing the same thing. Chicago was a magnet, pulling the young boy.

The faculty and staff voted. Richards faced the unpleasant task of writing Bix's parents that their son was no longer welcome at Lake Forest. Richards used the charge that the boy was too often out of his room after lights out in East Hall. That charge itself was enough for expulsion. He did not mention that Bix was drinking illegally. It seemed too much disgrace to add that to the letter of dismissal.

When Rendtorff took the news to Bix of his dismissal, the boy reacted with sadness. It was not sadness at leaving Lake Forest. It was sadness that he might have embarrassed the housemaster and caused undue trouble for anyone. It was never Bix's intention to cause anyone embarrassment or hardship.

Bix was eighteen. He had flunked out of one high school and been kicked out of another. What now? One thing was certain. He could not return to his family in Davenport. He had disgraced them enough.

With two suitcases in his hands and thirty dollars in his pockets, Bix took one last train trip south. The Chicago of the early 1920s was bumping and bouncing with motion, a sea of people in every size and color and shape, movin' and groovin' to a jazz rhythm. It seemed just the place for a wide-eyed cornet player from Davenport, Iowa.

Chapter Four

Opening Different Doors

No one knows exactly what thoughts filled the mind of Bix Beiderbecke as he rode the train from Lake Forest into Chicago that May day in 1922. He was not a person who kept a journal or diary. Even when he tried his hand at composing music, he jotted his own shorthand on the piano keyboard itself. On the cornet, he rarely played a song the same way twice. Always he tried improvising, adding a new bar or two, shifting a beat here and there.

But this time, as Bix rode the train into Chicago, things were different than before. There was no taking a train back to Lake Forest—or to Davenport, for that matter. What was that saying about "burning bridges"? Yes, that was what eighteen-year-old Bix Beiderbecke was doing—burning bridges to the past. Certainly, there were memories worth forgetting. There were those days in the classroom; the teachers' disappointed looks, the bad grades. Then there were his parents, who wanted so much from him and for him, and he could never give them what they wanted. If he could only have learned to read music, quality music, and learned to play something other than that—that—jazz stuff.

But for Bix, life WAS jazz. Living was holding that horn, cutting loose, reaching into the unknown and pulling in those sounds that reached into people, made them find feelings they didn't know they had. So many horn players tilted their horns up, reaching skyward, pointing into the heavens. Not Bix. He held his cornet down, aiming at the people, somehow aiming it at their feet, feet that could not stay still but had to be tapping or moving side to side. As he stepped off that train in Chicago in 1922, he wanted to find a spot where he could make the kind of music people loved. He wanted to play jazz.

The earlier night visits to the big city gave Bix a head start among Chicago musicians. After finding a cheap rooming house, he made the rounds looking for work. Surely somebody needed a piano and cornet player to fill out a group.

Bix had many favorite groups playing hot music. The New Orleans Rhythm Kings was one. King Oliver's Band was another, with Louie Armstrong playing a mean horn. And there was that wild but smooth cornetist, Emmet Hardy. Louise Panico was good. The Original Dixieland Jazz Band was tops.

But when Bix was asked to audition, to share a bit of his own music, he played like no one else. His music was his own, clear, sharp, phrasing that was his own voice, his own mood. Influences? Of course, he'd been influenced. Yet the sounds coming from the horn or piano he played were unique, strictly Beiderbecke. He had his own ear for sound, his own fingers and

The great King Oliver's Jazz Band brought the hot jazz of New Orleans north to Chicago. Oliver is standing, second from left. The young Louis Armstrong sits in the center holding his trumpet.

mouth. From the very beginning, he was his own musician.

When Bix looked up Bill Grimm in Chicago, good news awaited. Grimm's band, The Varsity Five, had played Lake Forest, and the two hit it off right away. Grimm told Bix that The Orpheum Theaters were looking for bands to fill their revue circuit. It could involve thirty-five straight weeks of steady work, of travel, and of cash coming in. Bix jumped at the chance. He quickly began to assemble a group and started rehearsals.

One night while they were practicing, a solitary figure appeared. Standing in the back of the auditorium, the graying fellow said nothing. But Bix recognized his father's silhouette. The boy went to his father quickly. When Bix returned, he shared sad news with his fellow instrumentalists. He was going back to Davenport. It was what his family wanted. The return to Davenport did not last long. There was simply nothing Bix wanted to do in the Mississippi River town. He lingered around the house a few days and visited a few high school buddies. The hours crawled along like the Mississippi River itself. Agatha and Bismark Beiderbecke did not want to torture their son, forcing him to live as a prisoner. Yet they did not want him a part of the life of drugs and wild parties that people talked about when they spoke of jazz music. When Bix asked to return to Chicago for the rest of the summer, they put up little argument. Just be careful, they warned, and never make the family ashamed.

Bix felt better about the situation. He knew he would never have his parents' blessing as a musician, not as long as he played jazz, and yet he desperately wanted their approval.

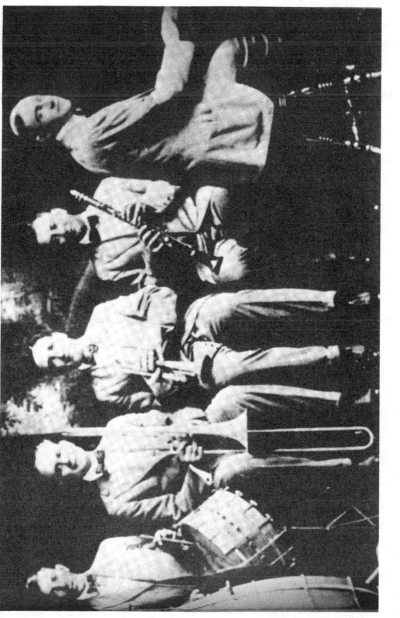

The Original Dixieland Jazz Band was the first white band to play jazz. Cornet player Nick La Rocca (center) influenced Bix's early playing.

Playing both piano and cornet, Bix enjoyed an advantage over other jazz musicians. He was easygoing, able to play with any group of instrumentalists and before any kind of audience. Whether he performed on a lake boat or in a dance hall, Bix won friends and applause instantly. The money was good too, fifty to seventy-five dollars a week. He got to travel, visiting towns and cities he had never heard of before. He even rode a train to play in New York City, where he got to see and hear the Original Dixieland Jazz Band, a group he had only heard on records.

At the end of August, Bix returned to Davenport. Agatha and Bismark Beiderbecke hoped their son had gotten the jazz playing out of his system after the three months in Chicago.

They were totally wrong. The summer had merely been an appetizer. Soon he was headed east again, ready to jump into the fast pace of new bookings. Each engagement gave Bix more experience and widened his audience. In October of 1923, he managed to get his professional musician's union card. Still unable to read a printed musical score, his playing seemed so polished he went unchallenged.

That November Bix teamed up with his first professional band. They were known as The Wolverines. With Bix playing lead cornet, the group included Jimmy Hartwell on clarinet, George Johnson on tenor sax, Dick Voynow on piano, Vic Morrow on drums, Min Leibrook on tuba, and Al Gandee on the trombone. The group meshed well together, achieving a rhythmic force and classy blend. Each member was capable of

By age twenty-one, Bix was a member of the Wolverines Orchestra. The group traveled the Midwest, filling up dance clubs. The members, left to right: Vic Moore (drums), George Johnson (tenor sax), Jimmy Hartwell (clarinet), Dick Voynow (piano), Bix (cornet), Al Gandee (trombone), Min Leibrook (sousaphone), and Bob Gillette (banjo).

carrying a solo, with Bix continuing to dazzle his audience on the cornet.

More and more of those audiences were college students, whose feet and bodies swung rhythmically to the jazz beat. Fraternities hired The Wolverines often, offering the band a chance to hopscotch across the Midwest. When they played at Indiana University in Bloomington, Bix made a close musical friend. His name was Hoagy Carmichael. A law student at the university, Hoagy was also an accomplished pianist. He sat in with many groups who visited the campus.

Once, while Hoagy was playing, Bix sneaked in unnoticed with his buddy George Johnson. Bix slipped his cornet from its case, put the mouthpiece to his lips, and cut loose.

"I almost jumped to the ceiling," Hoagy recalled. "Those notes were so beautiful, so clear. I stumbled over to the divan and collapsed. I had to catch my breath." Minutes later, George persuaded Hoagy to play the piano for Bix. Feeling quite confident, Hoagy agreed. After all, the piano was HIS instrument. After several minutes, Hoagy gave up his seat at the bench. Bix politely nodded, obviously pleased with Hoagy's performance. But when Bix slid onto the piano bench and began to play one of his own compositions, Hoagy once again headed to the divan. "I simply had to catch my breath again," he exclaimed. "It was a great revelation to me that the guy could play the piano as well as he could play the cornet."

Bix wrote to his parents, hoping they would share the excitement of his travels. They did not. In fact, Bismark.

Beiderbecke declared that if Bix was not going to continue his education, he should get a job. There was, of course, just the right position at the East Davenport Coal and Lumber Company.

In December of 1923, Bix gave the job a try. He weighed coal coming in, loaded it going out, and took financial deposits to the bank. It was a big change from playing cornet at a lakeside ballroom or dance hall. Bix missed his music, and when his Chicago friends started calling with attractive job offers, Bix begged his parents to let him go.

Reluctantly, Bismark and Agatha Beiderbecke agreed. Musical engagements came quickly. The Wolverines had to turn down offers because so many people wanted to hear them. Yet as 1924 opened, so did new doors. Bix Beiderbecke was destined to reach a whole new audience—on records.

Chapter Five

Perfect Timing

The Wolverines were hot! There was no doubt about it. Bookings rolled in constantly, and Bix kept his lip moving, the notes pouring out to please bigger and bigger audiences.

Whenever The Wolverines played on one college campus, there were students from other campuses attending the dances. Word spread quickly from place to place, and The Wolverines filled their booking calendar easily. They were dubbed "The White Men's Jazz Band."

With their name and fame spreading throughout the Midwest, The Wolverines took the next natural step for bands of the time. They decided to cut a record. Gennett Records out of Richmond, Indiana, was known for putting together quality products and was eager to put The Wolverines on a platter. Since they were all fans of the Original Dixieland Jazz Band, The Wolverines decided to record four of their tunes: "Fidgety Feet," "Lazy Daddy," "Sensation Rag," and "Jazz Me Blues."

For Bix, the recording session was both exciting and challenging. He was not yet twenty-one, and yet he was cutting a record of his favorite songs with a group he enjoyed. As usual, he was hard on himself and his playing.

Whenever he played, he was never quite satisfied. Perfect. He wanted every note to be perfect. It was like that all the time. He knew how the sound should be, but it never came out just the way he wanted. So often Bix would plop down on a stool and chair, his horn balanced on his knee, and he would think. Over and over he heard the music, note by note.

Finally, he would stand up and try again, once more reaching for perfection. When they were finished with that first recording, The Wolverines decided to drop "Lazy Daddy" and "Sensation Rag."

Bix was as satisfied as he could ever be, especially with "Jazz Me Blues," which featured him playing a rhythmic relaxed solo. Upon hearing the record, New Orleans trumpeter Bunk Johnson noted that "the boy plays like me, sometimes better." Praise did little to affect Bix. He just shrugged his shoulders and grinned.

Other musicians took note of The Wolverines as one record after another appeared. Bix's smooth, graceful style won him many admirers among his colleagues. They came to listen to "the new kid," the one with the Bb cornet who took a song, molded it into his own, and let fly. He had something special, something other cornet and trumpet players wanted, but never could get.

Bix's collection of "alligators" grew. Alligators were those music fans who edged as close to the band as they could get at a dance, swaying, swinging, sliding their feet and snapping their fingers to the rhythm. The college students were his biggest fans. Their own rebellious spirit seemed to be captured in the mood of Bix's playing. He loved listening to their chatter too. He might not have a high-school diploma, but it did not lessen his desire to know more. Of course, he knew and loved jazz—its players and composers. But his love for classical music, instilled by his mother, remained—and increased. Debussy, Stravinsky, MacDowell—Bix knew their work and could play it too. He enjoyed talk about Shakespeare; the British playwright's plays delighted him. From the wild antics of *A Midsummer Night's Dream* to the fearful misdeeds of a scheming *MacBeth*, Bix soaked up conversations during his breaks.

When time allowed, he read books by F. Scott Fitzgerald, the best-selling author who was capturing the "roar" of the 1920s. It had never been the learning that Bix resented; it was the structure of a classroom and the pressure of tests.

Not only did Bix enjoy the conversation of the college crowd; he liked their style of dressing too. He kept his hair combed just off of center to the left and sometimes sported a thin moustache. His dark eyes suggested a cool depth and intensity, his light skin an indication of time spent inside. Yet he welcomed a chance to swing a tennis racket or a baseball bat around, accepting any invitation that came his direction.

Hoagy Carmichael became a good friend, and he helped The Wolverines get bookings throughout the Midwest. Every weekend found them on a new college campus, while during the week

Bix's Rhythmn Jugglers take over the Gennett Recording studio on January 26, 1925. Left to right: Don Murray (clarinet), Howdy Quicksell (banjo), Tom Gargeno (drums), Paul Mertz (piano), Bix (cornet), and Tommy Dorsey (trombone).

they played in an Indianapolis nightclub. So impressed with The Wolverines and their growing following, Hoagy wrote a song just for them to record. "Riverboat Shuffle" allowed Bix a great chance to take the lead for some firm attacks with his cornet.

In September of 1924, The Wolverines headed east to Manhattan where they played at the Cinderella Ballroom on Broadway. The entertainment newspaper, *Variety*, labeled the group "a torrid unit, second to none." No longer were they just a regional group, enjoying a following in the Midwest.

In four months they'd cut seven records for Gennett, and people wanted more. No one questioned who held The Wolverines together. Bix was playing with strength and precision, attracting more and more attention among musicians and music lovers.

But Bix did not feel comfortable in New York. He missed the heartland and gave notice to The Wolverines that he would be leaving the band. He made a few more records with them in New York City, then headed west again.

Orchestra leader Jean Goldkette, operating out of Detroit, was interested in Bix. He had heard him play in New York, and he liked what he heard. When Goldkette offered Bix a contract, the cornetist accepted. But when the time came for Bix to actually play with the Goldkette band, trouble developed. He played like he always played, improvising, creating as he went along. His style and technique did not please those managing the Detroit operations.

Although this is the classic publicity photo of Bix, it was actually taken when he was only eighteen, on August 30, 1921.

Although Bix found problems satisfying the kingpins in the Detroit musical machine, he made quick friends with many of the other players. Tommy Dorsey, Howdy Quicksell, Don Murray—they were buddies to be trusted and musicians of the first order. When Bix finished up a composition called "Davenport Blues," he coaxed his friends to Richmond for a record cutting. It was the first known piece of many he would create, and he shared his unique timing, his fleet movement of fingers and hands, his genius of harmony. He led the other musicians, his style so secure and flourishes so brilliant.

But the Detroit hierarchy remained unimpressed. Bix was too revolutionary in his presentations, too individualistic in his style. He just didn't fit the mold of a musician in the Goldkette band.

What to do, what to do? Bix fumbled around for a few weeks, welcoming 1925 by hooking up with a few free-lance bands in the Midwest. By February, he decided to give formal education one more try. He enrolled at the University of Iowa in Iowa City. It was only sixty miles from Davenport, and he hoped to show his family he was truly serious about learning music.

But the plan failed. Bix wanted only to study music, nothing else. An academic counselor tried to persuade him to broaden his class load, take additional courses. Bix refused. Those high-school days of classroom assignments, of tests and projects, of teachers hovering over him, had left bitter memories. It was one thing to hear people talk about literature and current events, but

The summer of 1926 found Bix touring New England with the Jean Goldkette Band. In this on-the-road photo, Bix is seated fourth from left on the bus top.

it was quite another to discuss and write term papers, and all the rest. Only eighteen days after enrolling at Iowa, Bix packed his bags and headed back to Davenport.

His old room was waiting for Bix at 1934 Grand Avenue. When he announced he was going to take another try at piano lessons, his parents rejoiced. Maybe, just maybe, he could steer away from the corruptive jazz music. But that effort failed too— the instructor declaring "You know more than I do!"—and Bix headed back to Chicago.

For a musician like Bix, there was always a short engagement available. He was well known to other instrumentalists, both through his live bookings in the area and his records too. There were a couple weeks playing at the Paradise Inn, a week at the Rivera Hotel. Although Bix may not have hit it off with the top brass in Detroit, Jean Goldkette liked his work. He helped set Bix up playing with the Frank Trumbauer Band in St. Louis. Although Bix was always well received wherever he performed, he liked staying close to home. "Folks in the Midwest appreciate good jazz music," he wrote to a friend. "There's a special feeling about playing for the folks you came from." That was about as close as Bix came to being sentimental.

Sometimes fans clustered around him, wanting to enjoy the thrill of being near him. Young girls often tried to sneak into his hotel room or in the car in which he was riding. They screamed, cried, openly begged for his attention. It was awkward escaping their clutches. Not surprisingly, there were stories that Bix sometimes enjoyed spending time with young women, overnights even. They were certainly willing and available everywhere he went. But no one doubted that Bix had one major love—music.

Another of the Trumbauer band boys, Pee Wee Russell, handled the clarinet/alto sax like Bix handled the cornet. The duo teamed up to keep their audiences moving and grooving around the Arcadia Ballroom. Not only did Bix and Pee Wee delight the customers, they constantly jammed together after the band stopped playing. They added their own touches to countless pieces, and they encouraged other members of the band to do the same. Sometimes the band's manager would throw a fit about the new routines. "People expect us to play in a certain style, and you guys are always changing it!" Bix and Pee Wee smiled and went right on doing their thing. They even double dated two sisters, Ruth Schaeffer with Bix and Bess Schaeffer with Pee Wee.

They were good days for Bix, full of cheering fans and happy songs. The tones were full as he played, the jazz flowing as smoothly as the gin that seemed in endless supply. There was no drinking when he played; Bix kept that as a rule. Good music and good liquor were not a good mix. But after the people left and the band closed down, it was time for kicking back and relaxing.

Jamming for fun filled countless hours, and there was always someone there to keep his glass filled while he played. Inside of Bix Beiderbecke, there was a clock ticking, a timepiece that warned of danger. But he was too busy belting out the songs and belting away the booze to listen.

Chapter Six

Jammin' and Crammin'

Bix always carefully wrote the address on the package. How many times had he sent a new record he had made to his parents in Davenport? By the summer of 1926, there must have been ten or twelve titles. "Flock o' Blues," "I'm Glad," "Sensation," "Big Boy"—they were pouring out constantly, and Bix faithfully sent each recording home. But no family members ever wrote back with opinions or feelings about the music. Even criticism would be welcome. It was the deafening silence that hurt the most. Not being noticed at all. But Bix continued to mail Bismark and Agatha each of his records.

Bix and Pee Wee spent June through August on the shores of Hudson Lake in Indiana, playing with another Goldkette band. It was relaxing to play for tourists vacationing in the area and to catch up on some reading. Bix let his moustache grow a bit, enjoyed the conversation of visitors, played at the local dance hall at night, then headed to a cottage to continue playing and drinking the night into morning. He even played a little baseball and tennis.

By fall, Bix and Frankie Trumbauer were ready to tour as part of the first-string Goldkette band. Although Detroit music managers did not appreciate Bix's kind of jazz, many others did. Goldkette, himself, was happy to have Bix travel with any of his bands in the Midwest. They headed to New York City. This time a saxophone player named Bill Challis was a part of the troupe. Challis loved working out new jazz arrangements, streamlining a bar or phrase into a rhythmic collection of notes and melody.

Challis was challenged to follow Bix's lead, not an easy task because Bix never learned to read music. Every time Bix composed and played, it was a little bit different than the time before. It was a real challenge, but Challis recognized Bix's talent and knew it was worth the extra time and effort to work with him.

By October 1926, Bix and Bill Challis merged their talents with a song called "Idolizing," recorded on the Victor record label. It reflected a soft, sentimental style with Bix featured in a sixteen-bar verse.

Finding Challis was a big uplift for Bix. Challis could put together a selection that offered the cornet a chance to create and improvise. It was exactly what Bix needed. It allowed him freedom to do whatever he wanted.

Operating out of the Roseland Ballroom in New York City, the Goldkette band challenged other bands to musical competition. They were twelve white guys from the Midwest playing

Clarinetist Pee Wee Russell was one of the few musicians who could compete with Bix's vivid and rich musical imagination. This photo was taken years after Bix's death, during the Dixieland jazz revival of the 1940s.

music generally associated with black musicians from the South. But the Goldkette band had Bix Beiderbecke playing a hot cornet that never cooled down. Every night, customers jammed Roseland and pushed as close as they could get to the guy who aimed his instrument at them and belted away. No one went away disappointed.

Neither did Bix and Bill Challis disappoint the customers wanting good music on record. They reached a musical triumph with their Goldkette recording of "Clementine." Bix's cornet belted out chords that gave the selection power and substance. "Without Beiderbecke on his horn, the record is average," wrote one reviewer. "With Beiderbecke, the recording achieves a superior level, a record to be enjoyed and respected."

Bix produced a set of records under the Okeh label with Trumbauer in St. Louis. They were well received by jazz enthusiasts and other musicians, largely because Bix got to do what he did best—perform with few restrictions. The arrangements planned before the recording sessions were loose and flexible. Bix's playing had reached a point where the other musicians could simply follow his lead.

Wherever musicians played, whenever they talked, the name "Bix" came up. He was "hot"—known to anyone who had the slightest interest in music. With each of his records, with each engagement, his popularity increased. He accepted fame modestly, always changing the subject when people around him sang his praises. Instead, he would talk-up the other players, like

Bill Challis wrote arrangements for the Paul Whiteman Orchestra that often featured Bix's cornet at its best.

Armstrong. But despite Bix's focus on other players, his own following grew larger with each passing day.

The 1927 release of "Ostrich Walk," another record polished with Bill Challis, won immediate acclaim. Bix's sparkling and dramatic cornet passages reflected the talents of a full-fledged professional instrumentalist. He hit notes with a vitality and vigor seldom captured before. On its heels came a pair of records, "Three Blind Mice" and "Blue River," which highlighted Bix's whimsical humor showing through in sound. Confident with his talent, he attempted a few tricks with his composition, tricks that paid off.

Yet if there were any of his records that reflected Bix's inner feelings, it was "In a Mist." It was a piano piece composed over a period of years, added to and subtracted from, until finally a soft, piano solo emerged that captured a romantic mood, a sense of reaching but not quite finding. Despite the broken chords and fragmented bars, the selection suggested, the sounds reflected a warmth and tenderness of human hope.

Although Bix was performing mostly on his cornet by 1927, he put his piano fingers into motion for Bill Challis in "Candlelight," "Flashes," and "In the Dark." None repeated the artistry of "In a Mist," but they still shared a pure and simple charm. Although Bix favored black keys over white on the keyboard, these compositions were in the key of C. When his sheet music publisher, Robbins Music, brought them out, they were labeled "Bix Beiderbecke's Modern Piano Suite." The

Bix (left) and his friend Frank Trambauer, who followed him from the Goldkette band to the more famous Paul Whiteman Orchestra.

selections were his, and his name was respected and admired among everyone close to the music world.

In September of 1927, Bix cut his final piano recording, "Wringin' and Twistin'." It was a quick-moving number, once again soft and sweet, but it also seemed the composer and performer suspected it was the last time he'd record at the keyboard. He knew he would always love playing, but the horn was his first choice for performing and recording.

There was no denying Bix his rightful place with Goldkette in the home base Greystone Ballroom in Detroit. Like it or not, the top management had to accept the fellow they had turned away. He had become a major draw, a star whose playing pulled in the crowds.

When another Goldkette band, the McKinney Cotton Pickers, shared the spotlight at the Greystone, Bix swapped chairs with John Nesbitt. Nesbitt played a wild and hot trumpet himself. "If you love jazz," wrote a Detroit music critic, "and you get to hear Bix Beiderbecke and John Nesbitt play at the Greystone, you'd think you've gone to heaven. Those men heat up the night like no one else."

Professionally, Bix was on a high note. His playing was admired, his records were selling, and his fans couldn't seem to get enough. News that his old girlfriend Vera Cox back in Davenport had married another fellow left him saddened. She was always someone special—a girl who understood his love for music came first. But a few bottles of gin helped wash the

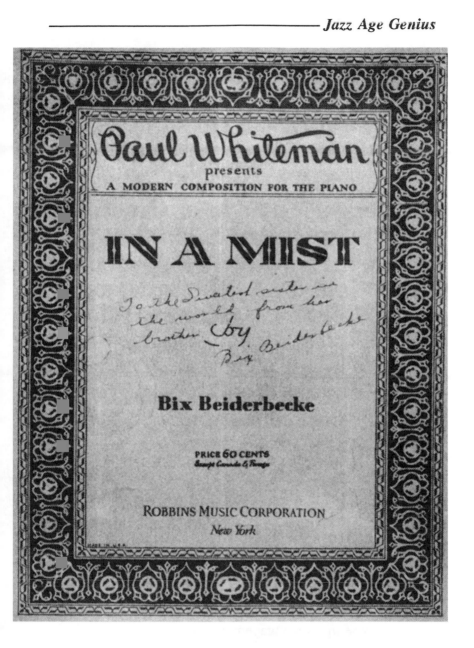

The title page from the haunting "In the Mist," probably Bix's most memorable piece of piano music.

hurt away.

Not only was Bix drinking more and more, he had picked up a collection of followers who never seemed to want to stop partying. "Come on, play us another number," was the constant request. Bix never said no, always enjoying playing and never wanting to disappoint anyone. When he did go to bed, he slept for only a few hours at a time, and it was time to get up and perform. He grabbed a bite here and a bite there, paying little attention to any kind of normal diet. Whenever he made it back to Davenport, his family scolded him, stunned by his unhealthy appearance. It confirmed their suspicions about jazz musicians, and Bix could not convince them that he never drank while performing. After the visits, it was good to get back to his buddies, where he would not be criticized.

Despite the success of the Goldkette band, finances ran short. Too many musicians getting too much money broke the budget. Once again, Bix was looking for work. He did not have to look far.

Paul Whiteman, a top bandleader known in music circles as "The Jazz King," grabbed him right up. He offered Bix $200 a week, knowing he was getting a top flight cornet player. Whiteman had a big orchestra, about thirty in all, and he enjoyed a fine reputation as both a conductor and all-around musician. Bix had always appreciated light concert music, and Whiteman included some in each engagement.

Excited about his new job, Bix called home and told his father

The famous Paul Whiteman Orchestra in 1928. Whiteman is standing. Bix is the third from the right in the back row.

about being asked by Whiteman to join the orchestra. Once again, there was ice on the other end of the line. As long as Bix was making money playing "that kind of music," Bismark Beiderbecke offered no support. Bix could have just as easily been a gangster as far as his father was concerned. The view from Davenport to the rest of the world was clouded and distorted.

Whiteman's style of performance demanded more of Bix. He had gotten so used to improvising, to being the solo lead on the horn, and now there were others who shared his position. If he did not perform well, he could be replaced. If Bix performed well, the Whiteman job offered financial security and an opportunity to play with a respected band.

Playing with Whiteman also offered a chance to make twelve-inch records. Bix worked with good friends, Bill Challis doing the arrangements and Hoagy Carmichael singing. The recording was cheerful and frisky, with Bix featured on several solo bits between the vocals. The jazz was light-hearted and fun, reaching beyond dedicated jazz music devotees to capture general music lovers. Bix Beiderbecke was a force to be reckoned with in the musical world, a genius of jazz. Yet he was never quite satisfied with his playing.

"He always thought he could be better," said Hoagy Carmichael. "Whenever he finished playing his horn, Bix thought he could do better than he did. I guess that's what made him a step above the rest of us."

Chapter Seven

Downhill Slide

Few of the Whiteman musicians paid attention to the morning rehearsal times posted. If the rehearsal sheet called for a 9 a.m. gathering, most of the players showed up at 10. There was a casual attitude about such matters, a lackadaisical feeling. The Whiteman troupe was not known for their early hours; often they jammed together long into the night. Early morning rehearsal times went ignored.

That was until Bix arrived. Bix might be sloppy about his eating and drinking habits, but when it came to music, he was dedicated. Whiteman had also picked up Bix's favorite arranger, Bill Challis, and he stood ready to help Bix any way he could.

Bix had broadened his music reading talents working with both Frank Trumbauer and Jean Goldkette, but the cornet player from Davenport, Iowa, had never become able to read a full musical score. Often, Challis merely gave his friend the melody and phrasing, and Bix played it back note by note. One time, that was all Bix needed, and he could master the most intricate selection.

Bing Crosby, one of Whiteman's top vocalists, was young and enjoyed vast public attention. He came to rehearsals when he chose, often being an hour or two late. But after Crosby heard Bix play, the singer's whole attitude changed.

A couple years younger than Bix, Crosby recognized the great talent of the cornetist. "I used my voice without a lot of thought to make the most of it," Crosby wrote later. "Bix made me feel more responsible for my talent, and that I needed to recognize that I owed my public my best efforts."

Crosby's respect for Beiderbecke changed his own discipline toward performing, and the vocalist's image rose in the eyes of the other Whiteman musicians and everyone who came to hear the band.

Most jazz bands cut records whenever and however they could. Whiteman preferred a well-planned operation, with contracts carefully established and recording sessions smooth and flowing.

Distribution was just as carefully organized, directed at a wider, more commercial market, rather than just to fans of a particular musical genre. Bix did not get as many solos, and the emphasis on jazz within the band slipped off a bit. Yet, playing with a muted horn pleased Bix, for he liked the sound that came out, something like a saxophone.

"Sweet Sue" became a quick favorite around the country, and when the band traveled, it got many requests. "Louisiana," "Ol' Man River," "Thou Swell," "Somebody Stole My Gal"—the

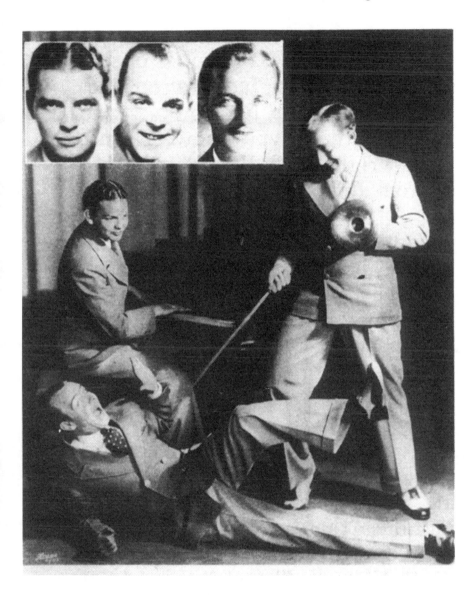

Bing Crosby, holding the sword in this gag photo, credited Bix with convincing him to take his talent more seriously. Crosby went on to have a highly successful singing and acting career.

records poured out. Bix, as usual, sent each one home to his family in Davenport.

The Whiteman Band used the Paramount Theatre on Broadway in New York as its home base. Yet, the group loved to take their show on the road. Traveling with the Whiteman troupe delighted Bix. For him, there was not the sadness of leaving a wife and children. He could pack a bag in ten minutes and be ready to head out for Buffalo, Cleveland, or Los Angeles. Chicago ranked high on his list of favorite stopping places because he knew the city so well. It was filled with old friends and boasted the reputation of being "the first city of jazz." The white bands played on the North Side, while the black bands played on the South Side.

When the Whiteman band finished its night playing at the Chicago Theatre or wherever they were performing in the Windy City, Bix never went home. It might be 2 a.m., but for Bix, that was too early to go to bed. The speakeasies called. A black singer named Bessie Smith belted out the blues in many Chicago clubs, and Bix followed her around like a panting dog. Sometimes tears rolled down his face as he sat wrapped up in her songs. One story goes that when she was going to quit early one night, Bix pulled all the money he had out of his pockets and put it on the table just to keep her singing.

Bix never passed up a chance to hear Louie Armstrong play either. Often, "Satchmo" entertained at the Savoy Club on the South Side. Bix entered, enjoying the warm greetings of the

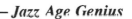

Bix once pulled all the money out of his pocket to convince Bessie Smith to keep singing the blues.

other musicians, and headed over to Armstrong. The black trumpet player would slip his mouthpiece off his horn and hand the instrument to Bix. Reaching in his pocket, Bix would retrieve his own mouthpiece and slip it on the horn. The music would fly as Bix took over, and a smiling Armstrong would wipe the sweat from his face and the tears from his eyes as he listened to another master perform.

The cross-country tours allowed countless Americans a chance to hear Paul Whiteman and his musical troupe. However, the crowds were not always calm. In Lincoln, Nebraska, a thirty-minute concert turned into a riot. Over five thousand people battled with police in an effort to glimpse the Jazz King and his band. Whiteman had buttons ripped off his coat, while Bix and the rest of the group were jostled and charged by fans.

Playing with the Whiteman band paid well, and Bix spent each paycheck with ease. Friends advised him to put a few dollars away for tough times, but Bix seldom heeded such advice. He was always willing to pick up the tab or treat an out-of-work musician to a hearty meal or a clean hotel room. Drummer Gene Krupa observed, "If you couldn't get along with Bix, you couldn't get along with anyone."

Many of the musicians in the Whiteman traveling troupe loved the thrill of flying. Only a year before, twenty-five-year-old Charles Lindbergh had flown across the Atlantic Ocean alone, infecting thousands of young Americans with "flying fever." The Whiteman organization purchased a streamlined Travelair plane to transport the musicians from place to place.

This photo of Bix was taken in 1927, when he was at the top of his musical powers.

Bix enjoyed flying, but he did not wish to become a pilot like many of the other band members.

People trailed around after Bix wherever the Whiteman troupe went. Some were music lovers and others were celebrity addicts. He could never say no when they asked for a song, and the promise to buy a drink was seldom refused.

While he played, Bix showed no signs of the alcohol he'd consumed. The notes were always clear and smooth. Somehow that horn in his hand gave him balance and strength, a clear head. But it was when he wasn't playing that he suffered.

Without rest and proper foods, his whole body collapsed. He saw images on his bedroom walls, snakes crawling up and down, bats flying through the air. They were typical visions for an alcoholic. A couple of days in the hospital would dry him out.

But by late 1928, Bix was worn out. Now he was the one showing up late for rehearsals, and his cornet did not share the same vigor and vitality of the past. He looked sloppy, and his playing matched his appearance. Paul Whiteman called Bix into his office and suggested the horn player take a rest—with pay. The holidays offered a good chance to spend some time with his family. Bix could come back when he was ready.

It was a sad Bix Beiderbecke who rode the train back to Davenport and climbed the front porch steps of 1934 Grand Avenue. At twenty-five, he looked ten years older, the result of too little sleep and too much drinking. He needed a rest. A good long rest.

In this photo Bix poses with bandmate Irving Friedman (left), Bix (center), and bandleader Paul Whiteman (right)

The holidays around Davenport gave Bix a chance to build up his strength. Little was said of his work. Surely there were times when Bix wanted to tell about the excitement of cutting a new record or sharing a stage with Louie Armstrong, but he knew better. When Bix took to the piano, it was to play Christmas carols minus the jazzy effects he might have wanted to add. Soft-spoken, respectful, always the gentleman—Bix craved his family's approval desperately.

The February 10, 1929, issue of the *Davenport Sunday Democrat* highlighted Bix's career and shared many of his own thoughts about jazz. "Jazz is musical humor," he stated. "The noun jazz describes a modern American technique for the playing of any music, accompanied by noise called harmony and interpolated musical effects." He went on to break jazz into two classifications, "sweet" and "hot," his own preference being "hot." According to Bix, "hot jazz" allowed for more pandemonium to break out in the music as opposed to the "purring respectability of the sweet jazz."

It was clear that Bix was proud of what he was doing in the world of music. It was equally clear that his parents were not. Once, while browsing around the house one day, Bix opened a closet door. There, on a wide shelf were all the records he had sent home—every one of them—in their original mailing boxes. Not a one had been opened.

When he rejoined the Whiteman band in February of 1929, Bix was refreshed and energetic. He needed to be. Not only was the Whiteman band playing constant engagements in theaters and ballrooms, they were playing on the radio, too. People could not get enough of their smooth and lively music.

But the hectic pace once again put Bix on a wild riding roller coaster. Recording sessions, live radio spots, performances every night—it was a lot to juggle, time wise, and once more he returned to his bad habits of too little sleep, irregular meals, and constant drinking. People smothered him with attention, always wanting him to play another song or drink another drink. Always the gentleman, the fellow wanting to please, Bix agreed. "Bix never wanted to hurt anyone's feelings," Hoagy Carmichael noted. "But you can let yourself be destroyed that way."

By the fall of 1929, Paul Whiteman felt he had to take action. There were too many nights of Bix's chair being empty and too many radio sessions missed. As talented as Bix was, Whiteman had a business to run and he could not treat any one of his performers in a special manner. In the fall of 1929, Bix boarded a train west. He hoped to rest up in Davenport and to return as a changed man.

The next months would change Bix Beiderbecke. As a matter of fact, the whole country would change. Both were headed on a crash course into disaster. The only difference was that the country would recover.

Chapter Eight

Dark Shadows

By now, when Bix returned to Davenport, he was a sick man. He had no desire to see old friends and confined himself to the family home. Some days, he did not leave his bed except to go to the bathroom. His legs ached and he felt weak.

Always wanting to maintain a proper public appearance, Bismark and Agatha Beiderbecke hoped rest, nutritional food, and no drinking would bring their son to better health. But it soon became obvious that Bix needed more than they could provide. He was an alcoholic. People seldom spoke of the disease at the time except in hushed whispers. But it was a fact no longer to be ignored.

On October 14, 1929, Burnie drove his brother to the Keeley Institute in Dwight, Illinois. Keeley was a highly respected center where alcoholism was treated as both a physical and a psychological disorder. Treatment called for immediate withdrawal of alcohol by the patient, followed by supportive care and relaxation. The Beiderbeckes were encouraged to write cheerful letters so as to hasten Bix's recovery.

Bix put himself totally into the care of the doctors. He was entered as a "severe" case, requiring dedicated attention. When he left the institute six weeks later for the 130-mile return trip to Davenport, the Keeley staff wished him well. Yet, they were not optimistic about the future.

Once he returned home, Bix welcomed calls and callers. They all begged for stories about the glamorous life in New York City, the recording sessions, about playing with Paul Whiteman. Modestly, Bix poured out tales of life in the entertainment world, always downplaying his own role in the activities.

Davenport boasted its share of dance halls and supper clubs where live bands performed. So did Rock Island and Moline, on the Illinois side of the Mississippi River. Bix usually left the house on Grand Avenue about sundown and returned about daybreak, greeting the morning milkmen on their deliveries. But he came home sober. Apparently, the Keeley staff had done its job well.

In October of 1929, the face of American business changed. For several weeks, Wall Street stock prices had shown a downward trend. But on October 24, panic broke out. People owning shares of companies sold their stocks, pulling their money out of secure businesses. One major financial corporation, The House of Morgan, pumped added money into United States Steel in an effort to stop the flow of selling. But the wave continued, and on October 29, sixteen million shares of stock were dumped. The results were immediate—banks and businesses closed, while people suddenly lost their jobs. The 1920s, which had entered like a lion roaring, became a forlorn cat with a muted growl. And the jazz music, which had added such vibrant and energetic accompaniment, seemed out of tune for people struggling to cope with survival.

Bix returned to New York, sober and eager to hook up with Paul Whiteman again. Despite the hard times, Bix was convinced there was a place for jazz in the lives of people. It was what they needed, sounds of spirit and strength, music to get themselves on their feet again. Bill Challis, Bix's old arranger, was delighted to see Bix feeling and looking so good. Everyone was.

Anyone who knew Bix liked him. It was as simple as that. Whiteman was due to arrive in Chicago in April. A movie was being made about his life called *King of Jazz*. There were last-minute items to tie together.

Bix waited in Chicago. He grew more and more nervous. For six months he'd gone without a drink. His mind felt clear and his body felt clean. He wanted to look good for his old friend and bandleader. He knew the bandleader might be cutting his group.

Each day brought news of people being laid off, out of work. The Depression had hit everyone hard, including entertainment people. Lots of folks didn't have extra money to go dancing or hear a band. Maybe Whiteman would not need him. Bix worried. Days slipped by. Still no Whiteman. As worry became panic, Bix kept calling people to locate Whiteman. Finally, he learned that the bandleader was headed back to New York City. Bix grabbed the first train he could get.

The reunion took place April 22. Whiteman was happy to see his old cornetist, especially since Bix looked better than ever. He soon found that his worries were unnecessary. Whiteman wanted Bix back in the band, as soon as possible. But wouldn't someone have to be cut?

"Bix, it's your chair," Whiteman answered. "It's been waiting for you. I want you back and I'll have you back anytime. But you have to be sure you want it. You can't say yes one day, and no, you're not sure the next. It'll be tough, but you can do it."

The words sounded great. They bolstered Bix, gave him new confidence. Yet within hours, the doubts were back. Could he keep up the pace? There were new recording contracts, the movie premiere of *King of Jazz.* More radio broadcasts. Another season playing at the Ziegfield Roof Ballroom. So many places, so much to do...

Bix returned to his room at the 44th Street Hotel in downtown Manhattan to think things over. Could he do it?

Whiteman was certain he could. Bix picked up a phone and started calling a few people. Maybe getting other opinions would help. At least, it would be good to mingle again.

Within hours, Bix was surrounded. It seemed like each one

brought a bottle. Some brought two. In the middle of the loud conversation, Bix toppled off the wagon. No doubt, it was only going to be a single drink at first. But that one tasted so good, there had to be another. Then one more...

Gradually, thoughts of rejoining Paul Whiteman slipped away. Now and then someone would call, needing a horn player for a night or two. Bix accepted. Jobs weren't that easy to get. But he wouldn't play with anyone. After all, he had some pride. Only two years before, he stood on the stage of Carnegie Hall, performing his own composition, "In a Mist," backed up by the Whiteman band, no less. Even when he wanted to sit down, the audience wouldn't let him. They wanted more, more. What had happened? Where had those days gone?

Bix's next door neighbor at the 44th Street Hotel was a young Columbia music student named Paquale Ciricillo. He, too, played the piano and cornet, and the two spent hours together jamming. When Ciricillo left for the summer, he loaned Bix his piano. Because Bix's bathroom was bigger than his bedroom, the piano found its home there. Guests were sometimes treated to a bathroom concert when Bix felt like enjoying the keyboard.

Another friend was baseball star Babe Ruth. Since his childhood, Bix loved baseball, and he enjoyed taking in a Yankees game when he could. When Ruth came into nightclubs where Bix was playing, the cornet player cast aside his usual shyness and visited the home-run hitter's table during the band breaks. Before long, they were sharing drinks and laughter.

Jimmy and Tommy Dorsey became good friends, too. Jimmy was a saxophone player, while Tommy played the trombone. Whenever they got a job, they called Bix. The car usually rocked with laughter while the trio headed to the engagement. But one night, the two brothers began arguing about how a certain song should be played. Before Bix knew what was happening, Tommy pulled the car to the side of the road and demanded that his brother step outside and settle the dispute with fists. Trying to play the mediator, Bix scrambled out of the car, too. Jimmy threw a punch, then his brother fired back. The fight was on! When there was a brief pause, Bix jumped between the two, only to catch a right swing to the jaw. The Dorsey brothers were shocked. If ever there was a peacemaker, it was Bix Beiderbecke. They both rushed to their friend's side and lifted him up. Rubbing his chin, Bix smiled. Within seconds, the three of them were laughing out loud. The argument dissolved into friendship.

"I'm just glad we didn't split Bix's lip," noted Tommy Dorsey later. "His fans would have run us out of town."

Despite not performing with Paul Whiteman, Bix maintained a wide audience. No one knew where he would pop up to play. Musicians stood loyal, calling him whenever they needed a cornet or piano player. He drank heavily but never when he performed. That was an unwritten code in his mind—a good musician might mix his drinks, yet he would never mix his playing with his booze.

Hoagy Carmichael remained a faithful friend, even calling Bix to make a record now and then. When they made "Barnacle Bill the Sailor," Bix showed flashes of his former playing, bright and spirited. It was like the old days, the glory times.

Bix's luck improved when NBC came to him and asked for his help producing a new radio show. "The New Camel Pleasure Hour" was a variety production featuring music and comedy sketches. The show producers remembered Bix from his playing with Jean Goldkette, appreciating his "modern style of playing plus a free, improvising type of music."

Not only did the radio show offer Bix a chance to play again regularly and pick up a weekly paycheck, it gave him renewed faith in himself. It gave him a chance to play with old friends too, top musicians like Lennie Hayton and Carl Kress. The players rehearsed often, giving Bix constant contact with his old buddies.

When the "The New Camel Pleasure Hour" debuted on the night of June 4, 1930, people responded enthusiastically. Bix played a lively "I've Found a New Baby" as well as some Bill Challis arrangements of "Strike Up the Band."

"The real power and strength of the program rests with the music," wrote one entertainment reviewer. "The Camel Pleasure Hour has people from New York City to Los Angeles tapping their feet and singing along."

Between the two major cities, in America's heartland, the folks of Davenport, Iowa, tapped and sang along, too. It was a special moment for Bix when Bismark and Agatha traveled to the NBC Studio B on Fifth Avenue to view a broadcast of the program. Bix introduced his parents to everyone on the radio set and at the recording station. Finally, he felt some acceptance, some recognition, from the people who counted most in this life.

The Bix style and sound could not be disguised. The Whiteman executives, some feeling betrayed since Bix did not return to them, did not want the cornetist recording for them at all. But top instrumentalists like Benny Goodman, Jack Teagarden, Gene Krupa and others wanted the best when they recorded, and they turned to Bix. He came and played, but his name was not listed among the recording artists performing. Yet his playing, despite less tone and luster of earlier days, still carried the Bix signature. That special touch still showed through.

The grueling rehearsals for the "The New Camel Pleasure Hour" began to take their toll on Bix. It was bland work, seldom giving him a chance to individualize, to improvise. Yet, never did his performing demand so much focus and time; he was spoiled, in that sense. He was accustomed to showing up, playing and leaving. The rehearsals in the NBC studio ran for hours. Bix started bringing a bottle of gin or scotch, hiding it in the men's bathroom, and grabbing a few swigs during breaks.

Then, Bix began skipping rehearsals altogether. It was too difficult to get up. Visitors still streamed into his apartment at any time, bringing a bottle and requesting a song or two. Nighttime drifted into morning. Bix reached for that Bb cornet and cut loose whenever he was asked.

Trombonist and singer Jack Teagarden was one of many who tried to help Bix during the last years of his tragic decline.

"They weren't really his friends, those people who came to see Bix towards the end," said bandleader and longtime pal Charlie Davis. "They were just people who knew Bix and wanted to use his good nature and hospitality. A friend would have seen the condition he was in and tried to help him. These folks just gave him a bottle and asked him to play. We should have helped more, looked after him. We knew he had a drinking problem, but we just didn't pay enough attention."

Towards the end of 1930, Bix headed home again to Davenport. He needed rest and always felt stronger and more refreshed after a few months at home. The Mississippi Valley area boasted more ballrooms and night spots featuring bands. Bix had little trouble picking up "one nighters" or "week longers" where he played cornet, piano or both. But this time, he drank too. Whether or not the Beiderbeckes confronted him about his drinking or not is unknown. Perhaps they simply chose to ignore the situation, feeling they had done all they could and that it was beyond their power to do more. Or perhaps, since Bix went out at dusk and returned before daybreak, they were unaware of his increased drinking. However, it seems hard to believe they would not have noticed. Certainly, Bix was showing signs, serious signs, of his failing condition.

Chapter Nine

The Music Stops

Early in 1931, Bix returned to New York City. He picked up a radio job or two, and when word got around he was back, he got calls for playing in a few bands. Tommy and Jimmy Dorsey booked him for a few engagements, Benny Goodman too.

But the work was less regular and word traveled around that Bix was irresponsible about showing up for bookings, and when he did, it was not the same pure music that flowed out of him. That finger magic on the horn, maneuvering those hands like no one else, those long full notes that poured out, the lighthearted dancing on piano keys, the gentle warm smile that accompanied each selection—they were moments of the past, never to return.

Suddenly, the folks at home heard there was a woman in Bix's life. It was the spring of 1931, and it appeared that thoughts of a young man's fancy had indeed turned to love.

The girl's name was Mary, Bix wrote, a native New Yorker who had never been out of the state. Red-headed and blue-eyed,

Bix referred to her as his "future wife."

Bix cut down on his drinking and spruced up his appearance. Clearly, Mary made a difference in his life. They went for long walks and to the movies. They went out for dinner, spending the rest of the evening in quiet conversation.

Late in July, Bix took Mary to dinner at Hoagy Carmichael's. Hoagy was flabbergasted at how well Bix looked. His skin color was good, his light moustache neatly trimmed, his suit pressed, his shoes polished. Hoagy and Mary had a drink, but Bix politely refused. Maybe, just maybe, things were looking up.

But the constant traffic flow to Bix's apartment at 605 44th Street Hotel continued. At all hours of the day and night, the vultures came, destroying any semblance of order and peace. If he'd have locked his door or told people to stay away or clear out—but that was not Bix Beiderbecke.

It was a hot summer, the kind of summer for which New York City is notorious. The streets baked under a sizzling sun, and within homes and apartments, people fought to stay cool. For Bix, that meant sleep. He only had a small bed, a bureau dresser, and a piano. It was the extra bodies that filled the space, unwanted guests and uninvited visitors.

Bix tried to break away. He stayed on the wagon, ignoring those who stopped by with full bottles. But the heat kept him awake, tossing and turning. The coughing wouldn't stop and the sneezing.

By the first week in August, Bix knew he was sick, really

sick. It was more than the reoccurring tonsillitis from which he suffered. He called a friend, rambled on and on about how he had failed in life, how he had squandered his talent.

Word circulated—Bix was in a bad way. No one knows whether any friends went to visit him. But the telephone wires burned with news of his illness. When Frank Trumbauer in Chicago got a call about Bix's condition, he called Davenport and talked to Bix's brother, Burnie. It was shortly before noon the morning of Thursday, August 6.

"You better get to New York," Trumbauer said. "Your brother is in trouble."

At first, Burnie seemed unconcerned. Bix was always getting himself into problems, often related to his drinking. Then he would pull himself together.

"Yeah, okay, Tram," Burnie answered. "I was planning to go East in a day or so."

"Damn it, not in a day or so. Now." Frank Trumbauer was not known to use strong language. And the tone in his voice was urgent.

"Okay, will do," Burnie answered. He put down the telephone and debated whether or not to tell his parents. Yes, his mother would want to go. Quickly, Burnie put the wheels in motion, booking two seats on the 3:40 afternoon train to New York City.

Sometime around 9 p.m. the same night, wild screams came from inside Room 605. George Kraslow, the rental agent for

Frank Trambauer, an amateur pilot, called the Beiderbecke family and told them they needed to hurry to New York.

the apartment building, hurried to Bix's room. The musician pulled Kraslow in, claiming there were two men under his bed wanting to kill him. Suddenly, Bix stopped short and collapsed. The agent gently lay Bix on his bed and hurried to call a doctor.

A doctor living in the building, James John Haberski, soon entered the room, his medical bag in hand. He examined the figure on the bed, and then turned to Kraslow. "I'm sorry. This boy is dead," the doctor said quietly.

Dead? Impossible! He was only twenty-eight. It couldn't be. He was too talented, too young, too energetic — no, it couldn't be.

Bismark Beiderbecke received a telegram in the night, informing him of his son's death. Agatha and Burnie did not learn of the death until Friday afternoon, when the train arrived in New York City. At about this time, Davenport residents received their afternoon issue of *The Davenport Democrat.*

The story of the cornetist's death received front page coverage. The picture of Bix was seven years old, the cornet player at twenty-one, wearing a tux, his horn poised prominently on his knee.

The cause of death was attributed to "lobar pneumonia" on the official certificate. Yet, Dr. Haberski, and other doctors as well, suggested the overuse of alcohol contributed to the fatality. Bix was known to consume up to three milk bottles full of gin and orange juice a day. His body just couldn't take it; his system gave out.

THE DAVEN
Weather Indication

SEVENTY-SIXTH YEAR—No. 259.   DAVENPORT,

CATHOLIC ORDERS

Harry Steeb, Moline Stud

PLANE FALLS 200 FEET AT LOCAL FIELD

DEAD IN NEW YORK

SEEK T MANY ON W

Accident Occurs Soon After Take-Off in Home-made Ship.

RECOVERY IS EXPECTED

Fracture of the Left Leg and Internal Injuries Received.

Pal of Fred B pital as Offi To Viev

Davenport Youth, Famed
As Master of Trumpet
Succumbs to Pneumonia

U. S. CHAMBER

Dies While Mother and Brother Are Speeding

The *Davenport Democrat* carried the story of Bix's death on the front page.

His mother and brother brought Bix back to Davenport for the last time. Services were held the following Tuesday at Oakdale Cemetery. The crowd was the largest to ever attend a funeral in the city. Hundreds of floral arrangements filled the Oakdale chapel, their rich colors brightening the summer day. A windup phonograph poured out the strains of "In a Mist" at the gravesite, while Davenport radio station WOC played Bix's records all day.

Of all the floral arrangements present at the services, none was more memorable than the one sent by Bix's old boss and good friend, Paul Whiteman. It was all roses, and formed a breathtaking six-foot tall cornet.

Epilog

Since the moment of Bix Beiderbecke's burial on August 11, 1931, his gravesite in Davenport, Iowa, has attracted countless visitors. Some of those who come do so out of respect for a musician who brought a bell-like tone from a cornet, who used his unorthodox fingering to achieve intensity and expression, who composed with fun and with mood, and who lifted jazz to a fine and respected music form. Others come out of curiosity, wondering how a person with so much talent could have let himself be used by others and abused by alcohol. But for whatever reason, they come, and they speak in muffled tones of a boy and young man who accomplished so much, and lost it, in so little time.

Among jazz enthusiasts, the name of Bix Beiderbecke is spoken with admiration, even awe, for he was among the "great ones" of the genre. His colleague and friend, Louie "Satchmo" Armstrong, once said, "There are plenty who tried to play like him, but there ain't none who been able to do it."

"Bix" festivals are held across the country, perhaps the most

The music stops.

elaborate in his hometown of Davenport. Each July, the Mississippi River town overflows with bands from the United States and beyond. They invade the giant bandshell in LeClaire Park, near the dock where a boy from Grand Avenue once came to hear the music. The air pumps and pulsates with the energy and melody of jazz.

Afterwards, the musicians gather to jam in area night spots. The festival includes a Bix marathon race that attracts over twenty thousand runners for a Saturday jaunt up and down the streets of the city.

As long as jazz lives, so will the memory of this young gifted musician who brought a bold and enduring sound to his life and times.

In November 1997 Bix was inducted into the International Jazz Hall of Fame. The cermonies were held in Tampa Bay, Florida, with composer and musician Steve Allen serving as master of cermonies.

"No one deserves this honor more than Bix Beiderbecke," observed Allen at the induction. "The notes that came out of his cornet gave the decade of the 1920s its own style and rhythm. As a performer, he helped lift jazz to its rightful place on the musical ladder. He truly created musical magic with his horn."

Timeline

1903	Born March 10 in Davenport, Iowa.
1908-1918	Attended Tyler Elementary School.
1918-1921	Attended Davenport High School
1921	Enrolled in Lake Forest Academy.
1922	Expelled from Lake Forest Academy in May.
1922-1923	Played in Chicago for numerous bands.
1923	Awarded a card of the American Federation of Musicians, Davenport Local 67 in October. Joined Wolverine Orchestra in November.
1924	Made first record on February 18 for Gennett. Left Wolverine Orchestra in October. Joined Jean Goldkette Orchestra in November. Left Jean Goldkette Orchestra in December.
1925	Enrolled at University of Iowa for three weeks. Played with Frank Trumbauer Orchestra.
1926	Played with Jean Goldkette Victor Recording Orchestra.

1927-1929	Played with Paul Whiteman Orchestra.
1929	Admitted to Keeley Institute for alcoholism.
1930	Played for Camel Pleasure Hour.
1930-1931	Freelanced with various bands.
1931	Died in New York City on August 6, age twenty-eight.

Bibliography

Berton, Ralph. *Remembering Bix: A Memoir of the Jazz Era.* New York: Harper & Row, 1974.

Burnett, James. *Bix Beiderbecke.* New York: Barnes, 1959.

Chilton, John. *Who's Who of Jazz.* New York: Chilton Book Company, 1972.

Evans, Phillip R. and Larry F. Kirr. *Tram: The Frank Trumbauer Story.* Metuchen, N.J.: Scarecrow Press, 1994.

Lees, Gene. *Jazz Lives: 100 Portraits in Jazz.* Buffalo, New York: Butterfly Books, 1992.

Sudhalter, Richard M. and Philip R. Evans. *Bix—Man & Legend.* New Rochelle, New York: Arlington House, 1974.

Wareing, Charles N. and George Garlick. *Bugles for Beiderbecke.* London: Sidgwick and Jackson, 1958.

Williams, Martin. *Jazz Heritage.* New York: Oxford University Press, 1985.

Index